More Praise for Goldberg–Variations

"Fly-fisher, word-hound, wit and storyteller, Charles Wyatt is most of all a poet with musical skills abounding. *Goldberg–Variations* is a vital symphony of poems, large and small, natural and artful, gathered from many years of devoted work. Wyatt unites his real experience as orchestral flutist, his practice as award-winning fiction writer, and his intricate sense of design, form, and variation to produce a masterful work where the even simple saying of a word is a musical feat as well as an etymologist's treat. At the heart of it all is his long title sequence, like no other I know, written virtually from inside the music and mind of Bach's great symphony. *Goldberg–Variations* is a virtuosity of verse." —DAVID BAKER

"Such delight, to spend an afternoon jiggering around in Charles Wyatt's *Goldberg–Variations*, within which we readers are transported to so many elsewheres (land of poetry and music; of Bach, of course; of Dickinson, Stevens, and Izaak Walton), each with its own lingo, its lush vocabulary. These are poems that love the language they find themselves in—its present and all its pasts, not to mention its vivid and raucous inventions. Wyatt's communion with words becomes a conversation first overheard then engaged in, as it draws us not only into itself but also into its world of creatures called by name. All the while, of course, we remain with Wyatt himself, safe and delighted in the voice he has constructed from the voices of all the best possible others, now become harmoniously his own." —KATHARINE COLES

"Walter Pater's famous maxim that all art aspires to the condition of music is given rapturous embodiment in Charles Wyatt's *Goldberg–Variations*, whose title alludes to perhaps the most triumphant piece of harpsichord music ever composed, Johann Sebastian Bach's orchestration of an aria with 30 variations. Both Bach's acoustical magnum opus and Wyatt's sonorous verbal accomplishment create harmony using a ground bass line melodically elaborated in the progression of a sequence, demonstrating that, as in genetics, there is no original form, but only a recursive set of variations. Ekphrastic poetry might be enjoying a surprising renaissance but Wyatt is the inheritor of an even rarer practice, call it auresis, or aural mimesis, that is poetry which imitates the pitch, rhythm and

dynamics of music. Listen closely, for enthralling the ear and stimulating the mind, *Goldberg–Variations* is a major concerto of a book, demonstrating the proximity of our art forms and the sheer universe of delight they can provoke within us."
—RAVI SHANKAR, 2014 CONTEST JUDGE

"Charles Wyatt's new collection begins with a series of introductory variations, from ones on creature-names in Izaak Walton's *The Compleat Angler* to lines from '13 Ways of Looking at a Blackbird'— all characterized by his stand-up's wit, Plath-level tropes, and linguistic virtuosity. Then comes the main event: his spellbinding poetic translation/interpretation of the Bach masterpiece that gives the book its title. In it, Wyatt combines music, poetry, fairy tale, myth, legend, and dream into what ultimately becomes a montage of the created and creating world. *Goldberg–Variations* is a book of marvels."
—WILLIAM TROWBRIDGE

ALSO BY CHARLES WYATT

Fiction

Listening to Mozart
(University of Iowa Press, 1995)

Falling Stones: the Spirit Autobiography of S. M. Jones
(Texas Review Press, 2002)

Swan of Tuonela
(Hanging Loose Press, 2006)

Poetry Chapbooks

A Girl Sleeping
(The Sow's Ear Poetry Review Chapbook Series, 2007)

Myomancy
(Finishing Line Press, 2009)

Angelicus ex Machina
(Finishing Line Press, 2013)

Series Editor: Andrea Selch

Design: Lesley Landis Designs
Cover Image: "Evening Bird" ©2014 by Luna Lee Ray
Author Photograph: Clark Thomas

The mission of Carolina Wren Press is to seek out, nurture and promote literary work by new and underrepresented writers, including women and people of color.

Carolina Wren Press is a 501(c)3 nonprofit organization supported in part by grants and generous individual donors. This publication was made possible by ongoing support made possible through gifts to the Durham Arts Council's United Arts Fund.

Library of Congress Cataloging-in-Publication Data

Wyatt, Charles.
[Poems. Selections]
Goldberg variations / Charles Wyatt.
   pages ; cm. -- (Poetry series ; #18)
ISBN 978-0-932112-72-9
I. Title.

PS3573.Y19A6 2015
811'.54--dc23

2015005988

Goldberg-Variations

Charles Wyatt

Poetry Series #18

CAROLINA WREN PRESS
Durham, North Carolina

for
CINDY

TABLE OF CONTENTS

WALTON POEMS

Worms

There are also divers other kinds of worms, which for color and shape
alter even as the ground out of which they are got; as the marsh-worm,
the tag-tail, the flag-worm, the dockworm... —IZAAK WALTON

Dragons I think these:
marsh-worm color of otter,
eyes full of fog, of glow bug,
but will not fly this creature.
Rather he will leap, his spines rattling.

The tag-tail is blue, a quirk
at the end of the bones he does not have.
He can be lured with a single feather,
even one brown of an owl.
He will come up to you
always from behind.

The flag-worm
is all cadenza – the orchestra in huge pause
behind him, a ruin of bows and one
dropped baton.
Oh he writhes like birdsong.
He is bouquet of worm,
a wind from the wrong woods.

Then dockworm sturdy
fellow miserable to be himself,
but he is fierce as winter,
as the ice he limps upon,
making of its spider-webbing
thunder – he cannot be found
until the fields slump with snow.
Fit through him the sharpest hook.

1

Feathers

Of these feathers we make the fumes of dreams –
Their heavy wings fold and spin –
All that ticks is not a clock, was not once
a child, a spirit, a haunted house, a hook.

Gerfalcon and Sacaret, grackles and the gentleman in black.
Evening beneath blue trees,
beneath a song of blue trees, of Bockeret,
of dog tooth moon wading the sky,

of the smooth stone above (beneath) Tassel-gentle,
both missile and missal, both mud and moss –
not Stanyel, not Ringtail, nor Raven, nor Buzzard,
Kite, Forked Kite, Bald Buzzard, mask of likeness –

We weave thee, feather, pluen, featherdriver, loosener,
feat feather, *looke how well my garments sit upon me.*
And out into the wind my line sends thee
to arrest a fish's dream of sky, unfeathered sky.

Who Dreams This Dreams Me

You may see the hog-fish, the dog-fish, the dolphin, the coney-fish,
the parrot-fish, the shark, the poison-fish, sword-fish, the salaman-
der, several sorts of barnacles, and Solan geese, the bird of Paradise,
such sorts of snakes, and such birds'-nests, and so various forms,
and so wonderfully made, as may beget wonder and amusement...
—IZAAK WALTON

Hog-fish, dog-fish, dolphin
Sunrise and dancing bells
Coney-fish, parrot-fish, shark
Blue evening's sarabande

Poison-fish, sword-fish
Shield-fish, gorget-fish
Cloud guitar and shadow fish
A small metal cannon

Salamander barnacle
The arrow, the arrowy
Arrow aisle unmerciful
Solan geese and bird least beautiful

But various and covering the earth with amusement,
and at table we dine on wonder,
on hats and cold potatoes, strum
the zither, shake out the halberds, the timpani,

the various, the nonessential, the phases and the tides –
an idea of snakes so knotted as to stir our wonder,
there in the galleries of the deeps,
great heaps of music meaning to move maestoso

to allegro to presto con brio, to net
the gold trombones, the black mincing oboe,
supple indifferent clarinet, fingers swimming –
kraken eying, this garden of hymns so dark,

the fishes passing in parade, unrhymed

Unnatural Fishermen

The otter, the cormorant, the bittern, the osprey, the sea-gull, the heron, the king-fisher, the gorara, the puet, the swan, goose, ducks, and the crabber, which some call the water-rat... —IZAAK WALTON

Upon the death of fish depend these occupations,
beneath the surface swallow-skimmed and light-reflected.
Instead of the clouds we see streaked there,
we watch, blooms of mud, eyes without shutters.

A hook jiggers by, quaint question mark, we watch,
shadow of wings, the ones that fold, the ones deployed,
chattering wide and narrow, never still, pages turning,
we watch, the cold mud our shelter, our moon.

That stalk has claws, the water-rat weaves contrails,
ducks, our cherubim, are painted on the air, the otter lazes.
On our pillow, ourselves – so many minnows minnowing
discourse of rivers – our spirit stays, our selves depart.

Flies

You are to know that there are so many sorts of flies as there be of fruits: the dun-fly, the stone-fly, the red-fly, the moor-fly, the tawny-fly, the shell-fly, the cloudy or blackish-fly, the flag-fly, the vine-fly; there be of flies, caterpillars, and canker-flies, and bear-flies; and indeed too many either for me to name, or for you to remember...
—IZAAK WALTON

There might of flies be a bouquet, a cloud, an element
that combines with air, with fire, even with wind.

There might of flies be a misery, a poetry, a climate
of buzz and bleat: mountainside-flies, spider-eye flies.

In the line, then, the fly alights in disguise, does not turn
himself around until too late. Around the lion

he may sport. He may devour period or comma – caesura
loveth he, and he may dash to love the place thought falters –

There might of flies some Latin be, some other name
known only to the doctors, the poets, the fisherman,

he with the line and pole, the thought of that he cannot see.
These words fly up, then settle down, then fly away.

No matter, the poem is spoiled and specked –
The room is empty save for in the corner one slight sound.

We do not hear it, but we know a web has caught one,
nothing so small to name and of consequence to remember.

Monsters

In the Indian Sea, the fish called the baloena, or whirlpool, is so long and broad as to take up more in length and breadth than two acres of ground; in the river Ganges, there be eels of thirty feet long; the people of Cadara make the timber for their houses of those fish-bones; there are sometimes a thousand of these great eels found wrapt or interwoven together...
—IZAAK WALTON

And in mind, a number may nest, never to forget itself,
made like music there to waltz, and mountains,
behind clouds, become small as mice, their winds squeak.

And in some country, the poem left-handed proclaims
but in another must be right – what country?
The one from which the moon may be seen – not where it falls

and sticks in the winter mud, singing bass below bass,
while the wind, still full of mice, cries farewell, cries welcome,
cries so be it, cries poor moon, cries that which may not be told:

Whirlpool, great eels, basket of bones, young bones and old;
down, whirlpool, or up – up sun, down moon, my left hand
is my right; thumbs, those twins, have come home, welcome

hands, number in the mind is two, now become three,
now growing; they write it down, but it falls into the sky,
mind in the sky, behind cloud, behind wine, behind bread,

and will not cry the call, not that mighty word, not ever.

EMILY POEMS

There's a certain slant of light

Imagine the chandeliers, the candles
at moonlight cant, hedge twist –

portrait of a pale cry,
animal rondo, puffed and pouted –

The orchestra files from the pit,
first the flutes, then an oboe,

cleaned with an owl's feather,
then several owls, struggling

with a guitar, a wheel of cheese,
the tiny bones and skulls –

They always leave because
they can see, they can sing in the

dark –

Rafter of satin and roof of stone

Stand the thing on end –
Now it is the figure of life
as well as a dead thing –

Let the animals and the ghosts
of animals gather around it
and sing with mumbling voices –

Can a table be a tomb?
Seated at his tomb – a poet
pauses – no – hastens to reflect –

The birds are the landscape,
scholars of the ground,
that hollow crown –

All the satin in paradise
smooths this thought,
statue leaning, the hard earth

waiting –

I dwell in Possibility –

In language, then – in the between –
the breath before the utterance of sound
and in the indrawn rhythm, the wheel turning –

The clock set deep in the air, neighbor to cloud,
to glitter of ice, of branch bolt shot
to earth to burrow, to burnt patch

where fairies elves goblins gathered
and ghosts turned their pages, mumbled
their sayings without breath without words –

There I stand behind thee always meaning
to be something other than you thought,
you turning these pages, remembering something

this –

Nor would I be a Poet

I would be the breathing of horses across the meadow.
I would be the rattle of these weeds
plucked from God's chin –

The self that waits in silence, become silence –
the ghost of a mouse, an apple seed in hand –
eye of the eye, seeing inside angels –

I would be this line, wedged like a fallen branch
in the tangles and folds, the shrugging center
of some essential poem, growing mushroom,

each crumb of earth shouldered, shifted –
and then I would not be anything – not
smoke, not dust, not one sparrow there, in the

light –

We dream – it is good we are dreaming

Say we are not dreaming – say
we play at being – the fly at the window,
the angel digging his dark hole –

wearing the mask of another day –
the mouse in the kitchen now another –
now imagination's mouse without

a thought without the good sense
of that yellow bird singing like a tea kettle –
singing the sky the sky no angels in

the sky –

WORDS

Glaver

The silence does glaver on,
spending its empty vowels
and dusty consonants.

I should flatter it
to give me even more
of its pleasure –

I'm half the rusty
railroad spike
(holding open this book

of old words) already.
I found it in my yard
once when I was digging

in the garden. Birds
made glaver over
me I failed to notice.

I reached into the dark earth,
roots and worms listening,
my hands closing

on that lost thing,
meaning to keep it,
to bring it now to you.

Malebouche

The adder rising to see in a rye field
flickers it – we have only Chekhov's
word for this, however.

The assailing crow, adrift on bad air,
abuses it – his opinions
never vary –

Very much wikkid tonge, black
air which settles on the night
steeps and bubbles burst

malodorous melodious bass
scrubbings, Beethovian viols –
I have seen the devil

and he holds in his elegant hand
before his tisking lips
baton light

as a sparrow's wing mobbing
another crow's awful singing
mal aria bad air

Buzznack

Such music as an old organ
might wheeze, whether pipe bag
or mouse-gnawed flute,

might limp, skitter and ooze,
might hover fogdamp,
curtain-wiped, carpet sodden,

an old machine like an old
lover, an old bull, solemn
in the far field, forlorn,

but its music gobbledy,
flawed, fancy as ash,
and never, alas, enough.

Beestings

Thick and clotted, the first milk of the calved cow
called also biest-milch, beesty, all curds and lumplets –

Small leap then to the sea when the earth has calved:
mer betee, lebermer, the loppered sea, a tongue

half lolled, and ears will never hear it drawing back
itself into the thin horizon before, batterfanged,

it hovers forth, hear now, flaw and nails, driftward,
awful as far as the beaten sky can see.

Ratt-Rime

From the elfmill, ear to the ground,
snake doors will do, hear it –
not that splurge of water rushing,

nor the turning wheels, earth clocks
clogged with stone, these rimes
rattle out rat in fatten fat hear it –

in the house that mast creak twist
moving midnight a lumped inch –
here's my bag of rats all fond

of piping rimed raddled ramfeezled –
rare readers my rats my flock earthed –
hear it spare hear it wraithed hear it –

a dead rat spells from the wall arat –
ferreted ratted now a cold scrap of
what was once ratt but now not that.

Lostling

They line up like moths on the window,
buoyed by the breath of dreams:
paper clips (trombones) and the trumpets
of spring flowers frost-felled;

a child perhaps, the one we (most
of us) have left behind,
shoes untied, ears before fallow
fields of unscrubbed dirt,

standing, perhaps, in a doorway,
hands clasped before, waiting for
the hint, the clue, that never came,
child we once were willingly

and then unhappily, and finally,
foundling, lost well, and no good
may come from remembering, that tune
so often poorly played, spilling out

images of which there are no photographs:
that worst of all haircuts, a bicycle
with fat tires, an unassembled flute,
parts in a bag, a heart, under a starry sky,

grown big as an acre of rose thorns,
knowing this pain was too large,
too noble, too naked to ever wander off,
and now we know it will not come,

so in the night we do not call,
content to number all lost things,
the small ones best, the broken,
the ones too shy to wake us.

Higgle

A little less than a little more
is still a little more,
and the pig higgled up
would have rattled the slop bucket
with its thoughtless snout
to make that empty
greedy sound –

To higgle down
ends in a skeleton,
skull in a window box,
vanitas.
And then tooth by tooth,
higgle farther,
higgle continents –

So the pig fattened
in increments of haggle,
slops being the natural
consequence of poverty,
the pig thus eaten
in the same degree
becomes a punch line,

the pig too good
to eat all at once,
porker limping on three legs,
or seven lines,
still sharp as a sudden
turn into the
wind.

Mirknight

The darkest hour can be counted,
but in a certain language, one in which
numbers are a single strand growing

like the light from a star hidden
inside stone wedged and crushed beneath,
but why go on? In the dark

it isn't even necessary to find shelter
because absence is enough and the call
of that creature was not intended for you.

Not a bird, you say, not a bird.
Something outside the dark, lost, too,
wanting in, wanting you.

Burdalone

Pushing the eggs out of the nest,
the brown bird stops to pant.
Even the storms that blow
ships among the hulking metaphors
gasp above sulking fishes.

Who is left then, last child,
unfledged, fledged, then failing,
bald as a cloud-washed boulder,
last yellow chick, following
in a line of one, faint crocodile,

its grim and cautious mother
stepping the cockstep on the dunghill,
henstep then and follow, fluttering
heart, old child, motherless pity,
father of many, of many meanings.

Bomullock

This is the bird which has no song,
which gapes and all the dark about you
falls in, falls in –

This is the face that has no eyes,
behind you now, and when you turn, behind
the paper on the wall –

This is the cry that stops your heart, knotted
and sudden, this, twisted brow where
no eye is watching –

mullach, mullach, the grisly ghost, yodeling
like a drafting line of geese, a goblin's
crooked eyebrow –

spectre of dark behind the falling snow
where the lost bird huddles and grass bones
melt through.

Larks-leers

Nothing but brush and snake spit
a countryside of air
water spout dust devil
sailing cloud shadows

There's no profit to be made of it
no good but in holes
and dry roots rustle
of some stray lizard

Only larks then nesting
where a song can scorch
the sun's eye shut
in wink or shrug

Conspiratorial waste
yonder beyond that hill
if you listen
you'll find the place

Knoup

Bells may be struck,
but clappered, they must rock
and teem out and down
like water from the wing
of a washing bird.

Here is the bell rope
which you may start with a shrug,
half a pull, hurple –
then the rest until rope groan
and bell cant pour out

belling toll alive and everywhere,
and bell pulls you up
into the din, clapper, hanger on,
knowing you must decide
wisely the letting go.

Haspenald

Think of elftall youth and of those
elvish verses Tolkein served al dente
and growing pains boy-grown
haggersnash.

Girls too will grass up wild onion
in drafty spring a short season
before the fill and fall of summer
houseleek,

and on the roof goats poise and prance,
higgle anything that parts the sod –
snakes fall but a child will grow
gatetall –

nothing so slow as age bringing
ground in view and longer songs
bent dragging fumbling for pennies
gnashhaggard.

Skainsmate

scurvy knave the bard knows what
the bard knows and skainsmate is soffet
to flurt-gils facia

why is it when we are not one thing
greed or rhetoric demands we must not
be two things

and why must the conjunction heading up
this flotilla of nomic ducks be struck so
soundly

and does this one answer the first lively
enough is it a little tune we whistle sing
or fart

that twinkles us through a night of sad dreams
and (that bell that coordinating conjunction that
skeinsmate)

stringing us oh scurvy knave away behind
along sad melody but dance and bend knees
of and and and

Dittology

Let us say a chance meeting at the well,
then dust, thirsty stranger, versation,
ablution, the washing of, more dust –

devil's smiles those gleams in sand
ants' footprints behind the clouds' lace
turn time's wheel a shoulder there –

then other deepmusing in brownstudy
other daw after nodding yes as if
disquixotted cat Latin arsony –

then slaked the story told twice
again dog's soup in the desert we
know our double stories well –

Myomancy

Perhaps there is only one mouse
and that we bait traps for it,
startle at the snap and carry

at arms length the sorry thing
dangling from its tail, still
serviceable in disposal mode,

to the dark mouse bin, and there
it transmogrifies, not into
footmen, or paper clips,

but more mice, of which,
in truth, there is only one –
the knowing mouse, the wise

and seeing mouse, neutrino
mouse, passing through the world
with mouse ease, blind mouse,

telling like Tiresias those beads
of fortune, moon-blink, we
cannot endure to see, sad mouse.

Mithe

In my mind small
place if world enough
with even weeds to hide in

I am concealed
and the difficulty is
in this seeking out of

me by me mornings
like this I've come from
where some dream perhaps

in one I was another fellow
whose nose was long a lie
it turned out in a long line

of mythy dreams me hiding
then and me seeking suddenly
a child's game in the weedy

world that wakes not wide
but narrow stark and even
dark the planet wintering

and I my company of me
too in walls of wood
then too in bone

my mes some slumbering
some up before the thought
that's almost never caught

Brustle

When the peacock flares
his bristles and all eyes

are open and upon us
there is a slow snick

an awful awakening
like thrashing through

cockleburs in the glade
at cockshut the hens

gathered in all fluffed
and broody dark

descending crepe
and bats tangled black

limbs brustling
through the wind

we hear it again
rustle on cold crust

of snow a lost leaf
lost mouse dog's paw

listen attend there
it is (near) again

Tyromancy

Knowing the world was not the goat's idea,
and the cow spoke only of simple things,
easily misled.

But the wide pasture ruffled under the wind,
and a distant skunk wandered and tacked
as if lost.

The curds like uncertain thoughts settled,
and the wise man regarded them, tomorrow's
poems,

yesterday's myomancy – the mouse follows
the cheese, the wise man waits upon the mouse,
the cheese,

the future, waits on the world turning one more
philosophy into the crumbs sated angels
leave behind.

KNOTS

Bowline

Not marlin or dauphin
but nautical enough –
a rope attached to
the weather leach
of a square sail –

leach leads to maggot,
of course, odd thought –
but the bow is a loop,
and this is a knot
that will not

slip the rabbit goes
into the hole
around and out –
little tunes these tangles –
small places

in the universe,
strings tied tight –
a hard spot in a light
air, the cut, the cran,
the grace of it.

Sheepshank

While I was trustworthy, loyal,
and certainly prepared
and could tie this knot
rapidly enough to win
a knot tying contest,

I did not consider,
standing there triumphant,
my tied knot cast on the floor
of the scout cabin
in my hometown's city park

above the caretaker's
tiny basement apartment,
who had one shrunken arm
and a wen like a large marble
protruding from his head,

and who seldom spoke,
but swept with brooms
he might have flown on,
and at that moment,
beneath our shouting

and my flourish like
a violinist at final chord,
sat silently, hands on knees –
I did not consider,
I am reminded to say,

what it was good for,
that knot – to shorten
a rope, he might have said,
pulling it into shape
with one hand against

his knee – or to save
the wounded or weak
part that time chafed –
Oh friendly, courteous, kind,
brave, clean, and reverent.

Clove Hitch

Not a dried flower bud,
the past tense of cleave,
nor a jerk or a twist –
The grocer ties a parcel
with its relatives
somewhere in the world
or perhaps in a book.
Behind me a ghost
reaches to place index
finger on the bight of
the knot (once bhyte
in the knotty old German –
bend or angle, think
of bow), and ghost or no,
I tie on, shuddering only
a little, not knowing
the one-hand hitch
which when I attempt
to tie (in music, to make
unbroken) falls apart –
is no more, as if
it, too, were ghost.

Cat-o'-Nine-Tails

A lively decoration,
five strand flat sinnet –
(braided cordage – think
old English bregdan,
a sudden movement).

There, the father of
the word meaning
to interweave
is named for the gesture,
the fluent motion,

of a woman's hand –
sinnet tapered and whipped.
The knob is a three-lead X
Four-bight X two-ply
Turks-Head leaving

between lashes hardly
enough time to contemplate
a sudden movement
neither tapered nor whipped –
tied over a manrope knot

which must serve as
the cat grasped in
the hand of a man
(in this story) decorating
another.

Bell-Ringer's Knot

Is actually the first half
of the ordinary sheepshank.

If it were the second half,
it would not be

(the knot being narrative,
a process, in fact)

itself, tied or arranged,
to keep the rope

from lying underfoot,
the bell, like the sleeping

dog, spending most of
its day in silence, hitched on

then, to this verse, untidy
though it may be, the

granny which if one end
is pulled will capsize

into two half hitches –
in this manner

the rope hangs beneath
its bell until such time

as it need be rung – simply
slip it loose and haul

the bell until the clapper
sinks into itself,

and all the dogs run
to the steeple and bay.

Snarl

Keep the snarl open and loose
at all times
using a pricker, bodkin, or stiletto,

and do not pull on the end.
No snarl
(from Middle English snare)

is too complicated to be solved by
this method.
Only patience is required –

from Middle English and French
and Latin we
untangle the word and find –

suffering.

THIRTEEN WAYS
OF LOOKING AT
WALLACE STEVENS

The blackbird sat in the cedar limbs.

The dog sat in the doorway.
The lamp sat in the hall.
A long time ago sat in once upon a time.
Saturday sat in Friday's lap.

Thunder sat uneasily upon the air
and slid off to the east.
Rain sat in the birdbath,
and one fat robin there sat.

Another day, another hat,
another hermit, another summer,
another angel, another gilded dromedary,
another flame in the garden

behind the birdbath behind
the watching dog and the long lit hall
in a time I can't recall even
wearing my thinking hat.

Say that it is a crude effect, black reds.

There in the wiry green of the rosebush, exactly,
black reds, shadows, neither rose mole nor
castor bean, perhaps home for the invisible worm

that crawls in the day – these are the roses I see –
not everybody sees what I see I have been told:
a bush load of dim reds, of black petals.

Dark matter is a dark matter and crude effect –
see Rembrandt pulling a customer away from
his painting – not so close, he cries – the eye

we do not share sees dew advancing in the air.
The other shuts – one world then, not two,
arranged neatly, if rudely, side by side.

And roamed there all the stupid afternoon.

Larks made passage in the air
over a sere and ruined place
where wheels of stone imagined
time allowed itself to turn.

The larks lit in nests of hair and ash –
even the cowbirds shied away
from that stupified company.
Dull bells hung and did not ring.

The afternoon's half opened eye
began to blink as if a lizard's tongue
had washed it clean, dim drear
waste of weed and rock, of web

and skuttle – sing then, poor lark,
cheerful if forlorn – a butterfly
clutters about, nearing your sphere
as if such things were meant to be.

That's it. The lover writes. The believer hears.

Two mourning doves under the feeder collaborate.
The earth contains their story, the tale of the trail
of bread crumbs and the children, lost chapter and

refrain: the little cottage in the clearing where birds
flare up, settle again, and the children skip and shout,
waking the witch, that unbeliever, old deaf woman.

But the earth believes the poet's world (birds speak
of it) and would have more mornings, more stirring –
even the fireflies forget to sleep and light the shadows.

That's it, then. All the creatures of night and day
compose their poems together, and the witch gnaws,
blind and deaf as any, to its marrow, an old song.

Stop at the terraces of mandolins.

There: terraces might be frets and to fret
over tuning, those same fifths on fifths
which rise out of the murk of Ravel's
Daphnis and Chloe ballet, would be poverty

of spirit, of mind. Once the tune is tuned,
we dance the dance of the caterpillar,
an untuned butterfly – with many minds
and butterflies in courses: bass butterfly,

octave butterfly, round-backed butterfly,
like so many tumbling leaves above the terraces
where we may stroll, you and I,
and listen to the yammering of the lin,

the doe, the man, and all around us,
a park, hawks in the air above the butterflies,
above the mandolins meaning only
to stop at meaning, to see, to plummet.

It is like a boat that has pulled away.

From the boat we see the land recede
and the harbor turns in a slow gesture
as our wake unfolds and we turn away –

And from the land we see the boat
become truer to the landscape, lakescape,
seascape, there a gull, there, the setting sun –

And cries of astonishment and applause
as it leaves behind one bright slice
broken free, sun bite, floating helplessly

until overtaken and lassoed by the boat,
and the boat, turning, steams or diesels
or sails toward shore where, waiting, we

stretch out our arms to the floating sun,
still yellow as gold and soft as a canary,
hissing and knocking sweetly as a boiling egg.

When, suddenly, the tree stood dazzling in the air.

Sometimes a wind, ignoring the other trees,
tousles the extreme upper branches like a hand
reaching down to pet a dog's head – a loose wind

rattling about in the heavens, lifting the birds
out of their trajectories, sifting through
the categories of birds, through all the bird

metaphors, word for word: a bird drank
at the stream, a bird struck its beak on the dead
branch, sound of sword, of struck branch,

but dazzling? The dazzling girl, my dazzling
thumb, a dazzling brace of trombones
hung from the branches of the tree, sudden

in their effect, chiming affably in the wind,
that loose French-speaking wind, scrambling
about the paper clips, the debonair trombones.

A sovereign, a souvenir, a sign.

The way morning rules its moving light
leaves nothing to remember – birds
fly through it. Large and solitary bees

climb it carefully – there is no taste of bee
nor bright sheen of sting, nor visitation
of spirit, angel, perhaps, equal to

the relief of sleep – toll it, then
sleep, bell, let it rock and bay,
give tongue to the rule of silence

and then slip away, past the growing
beanstalk, its sights set on revenge,
pot metal goose, tame ogre.

There were ghosts that returned to earth.

All the ghosts of grasshoppers climbed the same stalk
and there made ratchet music one by one.

In a story, then, someone to listen, perhaps the third sister,
who took one in her apron, big as a cat, and home

with her the ghostly grasshopper ratcheting some
nonsense about a spell and a second sister, but

I am the third sister said the third sister, and
the grasshopper climbed down a stalk and down

its root into the ground and down and down he climbed
until he came to the shores of an empty sea and

was transformed into a prince or a bear the third
sister can't recall as she sits at the kitchen table

sipping tea made from magic beans, weedy tea,
fragrant as the inside of an old euphonium.

The wind had seized the tree, and ha, and ha.

And up with its roots, hey ho.
And off with its prolific leaves.
Why should we say the wind knows a tree,
blind wind, blundering, entangled

in its own brash and billowing song?
There's wind in a river and wind in a stone.
There's wind in the last burnt bell,
in the night, in the word that names the thing.

Take the sword or swing the stick.
Break the sword and break the stick.
And ha and ho say the song through.
The dogs will play and the wind will bray,

and the tree in stony silence lie fallen,
feeling no calling to sing a ha or ho,
and the wind, long gone, has forgotten
the tree, neither flute nor guitar.

A crinkled paper makes a brilliant sound.

There is the sound of rising fifths on fifths.
The birds gathering over the whaleboat.
Its colors are blue and green poco a poco
crescendo.

There is the sound of pages turning by themselves.
All those sentences speaking to the empty room
until a single page holds still, giving a story al
niente.

And the room you've never visited, a passage somewhere
you've never followed, an indifferent door
which, opened, lets you hear the quiet fluttering
(andante)

of a thousand butterflies, mute, save for their wings,
which beat the air into a frothing cloud, and
there you stand, transfixed – from God's mouth. . .
(fine)

Even our shadows, their shadows,
no longer remain.

The narrow stairway
turns on its turns,
and the light from upstairs,
the room with dancing

and airs sung lightly,
follows only faintly,
the stairs dim
and the walls dim,

and the scale, l'escalier,
descends until those bass notes
so far away and dark,
lap about our knees,

and the shadows that swim
there peer up, reminding
a music to turn itself around –
the steps ascend

like so many things,
a melody at once remembered –
there at the top,
like a bare branch –

and one bird
which will not sing,
and the door to the lit room
is stuck and will not open.

Silence is a shape that has passed.

In a procession, horses, elephants, the wagons
colorful, and the wheels spinning, it would seem,
backward, the little man with the broom

following, applause, acrobats, candy flung
and falling, children scrambling after
marching music, all the several shapes

of brass bells mouthing rhythms heartier
than these – and then the sidewalks empty,
even where a tired child sat down in revolt,

wanting to be carried high above and who
would not want such a thing even when silence
comes last, marching in close step

with paper blowing, the sky a single
unmoving cloud, drained of color – who
would not want to march in step,

to follow, and then around that distant corner
where the lamp post stands under its unlit globe,
vanish like a lizard running on the wall –

GOLDBERG-VARIATIONS

Aria

A score floating before your eyes,
or the limbs of trees, some standing, some fallen.
It's more like something you've forgotten
and almost remembered – waking
from a dream at a sound and now it's impossible to tell
if the sound came from the waking world or the dream –
Bare feet on linoleum pass through the kitchen,
not bothering with any light.
The screen door opens with only modest complaints.
It is summertime and there's a piece of moon –
what do they call it – dog tooth moon, that's it,
and from the long grass, a soft seething of crickets –
from farther off, something which you might recognize as frogs –
do you remember this, the woods opening like the pages of a book?
You're riding the back of something not a horse,
something with a gait of twelve steps, undulating the while.

Then a clearing and the moon is half buried in the forest,
its light almost blinding. A rabbit ignores you,
eating clover in the clearing, its head long like a deer's.
You are alone. The moon is fading. You're walking
through the house and each room darkens as you approach.
The house has as many rooms as trees have leaves
and some of them are falling. Together
you fall and the world falls so there is no sensation
of falling because the bass line is rising
and there are keys under your fingers.
Touch is all that matters.
You are alone. The moon is fading.
There are a thousand keys in as many rooms.
The strings are waiting, holding every sound.
You are alone.
In a moment, something will touch you.

You'll wake again.

Variation 1

Once an evil stepmother killed her stepson
by knocking off his head with the lid of a box.
She made him into a stew, which she fed to his father
and the gathered bones
his sister placed at the base of a juniper tree.

From the tree arose flames
and from the flames a beautiful bird appeared.
And the bird sang a song: this song:
And this song the bird traded for a gold chain and red slippers
and finally a huge millstone through the center of which
the bird thrust its neck and flew to a rooftop
where it began to sing even more beautifully.

It gave the gold chain to the father,
the dancing slippers to the sister,
and it dropped the millstone
on the head of the stepmother.
"What a fine bird," it sang.

In some stories the bird transforms itself into the lost brother.
In some the bird continues to sing,
never pausing to trade with mortals
for reward or revenge.

This is an old room, isn't it, the door of which
we've opened together: that bird singing,
flames rising beneath the juniper tree.
There is scarcely time for a breath.

Variation 2

A cat guards the front
          door of the gingerbread house,
so we must go around to the back
          and nibble on the woodshed.

Hansel's finger plays the bass notes,
          chicken bone though it is.
The witch will not see you
          unless you move,

but who can resist the dance?
          Toe tapping all the way
to the cage and then there's nothing
          for it but to push

the old lady in the oven. The crone's cat,
          still resting on the porch,
rolls over on its back,
          dreaming of candied mice.

The forest is ankle deep in bread crumbs.
          There is the faint smell
of baking witch, not unpleasant,
          like apple pie.

Variation 3

The king's son must marry some sister –
The third sister from the attic is chosen by the tree
which grew from her golden laughter.

Of course, the first and second sisters gouge out
her eyes, cut off her hands, and lock her in the attic,
the third sister.

One day she feels a snake wrap around her legs,
the snake under the bed. More snake magic
to bargain from the king

both eyes and hands, her own. (Only in stories
are gouged eyes and hacked hands kept safe).
Restored, the third sister;

and burned at the stake, the two wicked sisters
and the scorpion one gave birth to; and
on the same day, a wedding;

but of the snake, canon at the unison,
12/8 in the key of G, twice eight measures,
telling the same tale over and never –

of the snake under the bed,
home from the woods in her apron,
no one knows, not even the third sister.

Variation 4

Heart of the heart of the harpsichord.
Hands arched from nearly below the keyboard.
Strings plucked but there is an element of touch.
You can hear it.

Moths on the window bellied up.
A four note figure crowded upon itself passing in parade.
This is not the first time.
There is no first time, no once upon a time, or twice beneath.

All those moths dreaming of flying, each one a note.
You're waiting for one, but which one?
The train is passing – you wait, ignoring the signal bell,

your basket of hacked hands and gouged eyes on the seat beside you.
If the world would only let you be on time.

Variation 5

(with repeats)

moth on the glass and the'
moth on the window screen
ever so lightly my fingers

on the screen and the moth flies up
lighter than my fingers
this is the moth

both unbidden and inevitable
a curving streak toward and away
from the light curving

like the edges of the shouldering moon
but the moth on the glass
grows larger in its waiting

something more important is coming
than this thin drumming of my fingers
these fingers drumming upon the keyboards

never stopping to breathe hands on knees
these are fingers and the moths are flying
beyond waiting but also

moon reaching through the glass
the moth in the night and the

(da capo)

Variation 6

Canone alla Seconda

From the moths to a clutch of dead
souls
dancing wildly in a church,

the church beyond the sunken
moon,
glowing at mirknight.

What gift have you brought them?
Lively
souls dancing in three circles –

you have no gift?
Then
let them take you into their circle,

and they'll let you go afterward
if
you follow in the dance, one step behind,

making a strange but perfect
music.
What gift have they for you?

You'll see soon enough – don't miss your
step –
a piece of moon, smelling like cantaloupe,

bright itself as your eyes are dark,
dark
as the dust under the church floorboards

where the hacked hands and gouged
eyes
are kept in neat muslin sacks. Keep in step

one step behind, a dark step, careful step,
following
the step one degree before, a falling step –

the candle light is flickering.

Variation 7

al tempo di Giga

Through it with a bell
a small bell to light the bats
the moth ladies home

the time of dream
waters   from beneath mountains
risen out and sliding down

not cheerfully but noise
like a wind and this
we sail upon

dream not shaped
by us   ferns grown over
and mist sharpens

then bears and tall horses
moths drop their wings
angel into the earth

moss bears bring more bells
and we plant in them
candles   keys   a drop of blood

one last light dim torch
held in the hand
that once   was yours

Variation 8

a 2 Clav.

The principle of contrary motion typically
involves a descending pattern in the right hand
and an ascending pattern in the left.

The ear is further satisfied by the juxtaposition
of eighths against sixteenths – what a fine bird am I.

the pattern may be reversed and inverted:
Truth may follow beauty – the gold chain,
or beauty follow – red slippers.

Crow bearing into wind may rise or fall,
perhaps hold steady,
laboring through nothing else save time.

Beneath, a wheatfield seethes – *from one keyboard,*
painting the wind with flung sun – *to the other.*

Hear in its voices a chorus of thousands.
By itself the wind has no voice at all,
only intent: falling – *the millstone.*

How can rising voices sound? *At some cost*
says the adder – raising its head above
the bending wheat stalks.

How then says the curling smoke which the wind
shreds like a dog shaking the adder.

Silence now as certain (cadence in G)
as if it had always been – in the time of a thought,
an hour of waiting, a single moment,

flames rising from the juniper tree,
a breath drawn in.

74

Variation 9

You're riding the back of something not a horse,
something with a gait of eight steps, undulating the while.
It's always night in the score, among the waiting strings,

and only the struck strings are visible, like vines.
Always a moonlit sheen to the visible and to the invisible –
a feeling, like plush or deep moss.

The moon will rise in the cadence and you'll see the creature
which seems to be a milkweed caterpillar
and it's a leaf you're sailing on,

very much like a smooth sea.
Say there are three daughters, and two
have already been hacked to pieces by the evil sorcerer.

But the story will be in that third daughter.
Begun in the canon at the third.
The caterpillar, already enormous, is growing,

but the fine saddle you have been provided
is causing it no apparent discomfort.
The cadence is coming and you realize

the pitches have been bells
and that there is something keener than pitch
just as the moon heaves up

and the world is a harpsichord.

Variation 10

Fughetta

Put the two ugly stepsisters in a barrel laced
with spikes
and roll it down the hill into the river – thus ends
an older variant of Cinderella.

This rolling barrel, then, creates the subject
of its fugue,
a blend of cascading and bouncing. The bounces
create the space –

roll it down the hill into the river – the space which
will be filled
later on by the movement of the secondary voices
(perhaps the voices

of the stepsisters, performing, finally, a useful function)
and this fugue
is a thousand glass slippers, each fitting perfectly.
Roll it down,
now with a countermelody and all of four voices,

the two sisters (*good riddance*, says the storyteller),
and the Prince and C,
about to enter the land of Ever After, the lost land.
They say

it is a happy land, but no one has ever returned from it.
Perhaps that is
because it is a happy land. Perhaps (in all four voices).
The barrel

takes a last leap toward the cadence.

Variation 11

In this landscape, music
is the swarming of gnats,
not the gnats themselves,
but their tight and determined
meandering.

Only in this music is
the motion evident, its order
and precision, the choices one
of its paths leaves to the others.

A hawk falls out of its floating watchfulness
like a mortar shell.
A snake strikes after a careless footfall –
direction – trajectory – decision.
In a story,

a king has three daughters,
or a poor man has one.
One day, the hunter's dog
turns and speaks to him.

There has been a careless shuffling
of seasons, or days.
The dog speaks of buried gold.
And together, dog and hunter
dig into the earth,

sending up geysers of soil and dust.
Now the shovel and pick and
claws strike hard stone.
Descending triplets:

the dog's two digging legs,
the hunter's implement.
The gold forgotten, they dig.

Stars shower down
from the night above them.
Everything is falling.

Variation 12

Canone alla Quarta

Left-handed, and in contrary motion.
Imagine a second Hansel choosing always

the leftward branch of the woody labyrinth
while the first chooses always the right.

Floating over a free bass at the interval
of a fourth, the maze attends only to itself.

This one has no center, no Minotaur,
just the dark hillside and the path

obliterated in ferns, the children lost forever.
But then, it might all have been a dream,

a feather floating down, perhaps a pink ribbon,
the forest drained of its chaos – and in the distance,

faintly, a single bird, wood thrush, singing.

Variation 13

The melody floating over a descending bass –
you wake from it and it is forgotten again,
but you know you can't sleep.

Bare feet on linoleum, on the hard wood of the library,
on cold stones cobbled like a carapace, on moss,
and then, rising, on moonlight, owl-lit,

the night beneath, mice pausing in their labors,
shadow passing, weighty shadows passing,
the third sister, left by the sorcerer, inside his splendid house,

with a key and an egg and, of course, a forbidden door,
frog song filling the low places, a whippoorwill
counting its questions, moth patience,

the abandoned children shouldering through
mushrooms and underbrush, their faint cries
sounding oddly like laughter,

there, in the eye of the firefly, everything reflected,
understood, repeated, forgotten, the triple-flagged thirty-seconds
circling themselves, the E flat in the bass

a large round stone, smooth roof over some other world.

Variation 14

a 2 Clav.

How many magic beans make five,
a strange old man asks Jack
who answers (no simpleton he, sharp as a tack)
two in each hand and one in your mouth –

but after trading the white cow for them,
Jack suffers from magic bean remorse
and throws them in the air.

Five times five hundred trilling beans
the beanstalk bears before Jack

chops it with his mother's ax –
and what of Fee-fi-fo-fum, or
Fie, foh, and fume, or (in Welsh)
Fee, fau, fum? Says Jack, *Fie.*

More beans, then, more magic gathering,
and the ogre, fallen like the moon
and wedged into the earth

deeper than any roots – more trills
than beans, than beans' magic,

more than stars, more than two
hands can hold, more fingers
than hands – faster than sand
falling to measure time's measure,

more than one white cow, however milky.
How many beans make six,
a strange old man sent up

from the musing of the earth
asks another Jack (again, no simpleton).

No fool. (Hands crossing.)

No wonder.

Variation 15

Canone alla Quinta

Her slumber spreads a cloud throughout the castle:
The Beauty of the Sleeping Forest, Briar Rose,
Snow White, Goldilocks in the smallest bed.

And in g minor the canon speaks inverse over a bass
that prowls the castle, searching vine-like up the stairs
for the highest room, rusting key (minor) in the door

to the room where a dozen maidens weave a tapestry
that spills out the window into the world,
and all the shapes and fairies, all the witches

and ogres spill into the void: prince, faithful dog,
third sister, the path under the dark arch of trees
leading to the castle where the bass prowls

and the maidens spin out the world, its landscape
the silent shape between voices of the canon
at the fifth where if the first voice rises,

the second must fall: thus mountains and fish
of the seas, the slow flight of birds and clouds
in steps, slow steps, this the maidens spin in sleep:

one turn will shape the world, the minor key that
sleeps a hundred years, world that spins itself
and step by step ascends to the small door

whose rusting key begins to turn. . .

Variation 16

Ouverture

In the French style,
        bristling with dotted rhythms
and thirty-second pickups
        (in bouquets of three),

giving the general impression
        of a leaf or scrap of paper
blowing and tumbling furiously
        in the wind, only touching ground

occasionally, and like all ouvertures,
        breaking into something more
down-to-earth, in this case,
        not a fugato, but a dance:

In the forbidden room, then,
        a huge bowl of blood
        and hacked body parts –

the third sister assembles her two siblings:
        head, body, arms, legs,
        ouverture, dance, coda –

or the witch who called
        for a bottle of Snow White's blood,
        stoppered with her toe –

in the shadow of Bluebeard's castle,
        out of the fingers, then, into the air,
        this maggot called harpsichord,

strung and levered, which transforms
        what mind hears upside down
        into that which mind hears

righted, and stories that begin in once
        and end in after, passing through
        measures of middle,

of cadenza, of mordant,
        grupetto and trill,
        under the shrouded moon.

Variation 17

Night is a study in thirds
        (and sometimes sixths)
                arranged in stairsteps.

A castle looms in moonlight,
        its towers dark
                against lit clouds.

A great curving
        staircase sweeps around
                the hillside and a

beautiful maiden hurries
        downward, her hand
                brushing the stone wall.

But in the musical castle,
        she can hurry upward
                with the same speed and grace.

Is she hurrying to meet her lover,
        or is she fleeing from
                some misshapen troll?

Perhaps it is she herself who
        will be transformed
                the moment the moon

clears the eastern turret.
        There are always three
                daughters, two sisters,

one king and half a prince.
        Here there are a hundred maidens
                hurrying up and down the staircases.

The hill has become a mountain and
      the stairs themselves
            are moving like water.

A single owl releases its grip
      and launches itself into the
            silence of the cadence.

Variation 18

a 1 Clav.
Cannone alla Sesta

Here there is no darkness, no earth,
no roots, no hidden tangles of serpents –
the bass is free, not planted, not framed, alone

in what is not day or night or even air,
and over it two voices sail, the second
an echo at the sixth of the first. If

there were ocean, it would part; if there
were forest, it would fade; if there were moon –
always this healing, the hacked sisters hidden

in a bag of gold, hauled by the ensorcered
sorcerer to their own home while the third sister,
covered in honey, rolls in the bed's feathers

and becomes a fabulous bird – if there were moon,
this would be its music, the single creature
of the world, its myriad legs working, its

two-winged voices sailing – into itself,
through itself, emerging from itself.
A time then, and twice upon it, some such music

(this precise music following itself),
and its end, the end of time, the end
of ending, but not, but not of counting.

Variation 19

This is the clock a mouse made.
Larks fly through it –
the wheels, though mouse made,
wheel grandly, windmill wheels,
the mill grinding, the wind wheeling
over a land so poor only the larks nest there.

The mice have long abandoned this place,
taking their stories of cleavers and knives,
of ax and spear, of shoebox and sardine tin,
of cat bells and gnawed molding, leaving
something of purring in the smallest clock wheels –

these are the sixteenths and they turn on themselves,
almost committing to a mouse-like journey.
Beyond the clock is another clock
and at a great distance, this cannone alla sesta.
Some wheels turn so slowly, the larks nest in them,
but they must flare up when time runs out.

Variation 20

Sparrows now, and hands crossing,
a ringing rain in which two voices become one –
there in that wall of ivy, dozens of them,
gregarious, combative, a square dance
of sparrows, bar brawl, swooping and unmusical,
and the ivy wall, not straw, or twigs, but brick,

windy sparrows,
and the wolf beneath wandering from story to story,
hunting, haunted, swallowing
whole variations and coughing them like a cat –
returned, they are faster, more compact,

keener, sparrows now bees in a world of triplets,
the wolf driven away, dingo, jackal,
serpent, limping fox, buzzing string,
ringing silence.

Variation 21

Cannone alla Settima

The fence wire at its top is barbed,
a double turn at intervals like bar lines.
The color of this and the pattern below
is rust, but not a polleny rust,
a deep blood rust, more brown than red –
and the squares are stretched here into bricks
never to be made whole again, held
always by this post and the others,
like the moon one side lichened white,
white as bird lime and the rest gray,
rain gray and a little twisted,
but this is all to see through
This is the cow you'll trade for beans –
but here at your feet, brighter than the sun
you can feel warming your back,
these thousand buttercups, yellow –
they eat yellow – yellow, they make love
to yellow – yellow, they make the
white cow pulling up the cool wet grass
in soft regular crunching tears
while her calf slips sometimes sucking
and that only you can hear
as a subtone behind the mother –
they make her, the buttercups make her,
remember, the white cow
and her calf *(in g minor)*
this in the green grass
with, only at the base of this fence
post, half of a dandelion gone to seed.

Variation 22

Here the struck sound / which is:
light through the gnawed leaf. And again.
Every bird of the wide places:

jay, sparrow, lark, swallow, and again,
scissors shaping the cloth, and again, of air.
From the language of gnawed leaf,

struck sound, and again,
strike it until its first meaning has flown: and again,
crocodile, anodyne, porcelain, and again,

and again, light flaring its waves and particles,
take a steely tempo, lively but stately still (and again)
and the leaf dissolves in light, look into the sun

(not for the tied halves but for the struck edge of an eighth):
the third sister become the magic bird has left a skull
adorned with jewelry and flowers grinning from an attic window

to welcome the sorcerer to his wedding feast.
Bird to sorcerer: she has swept the house and awaits you:
look : here : and again.

The air confused by yellow butterflies
and a scattering of jay, sparrow, lark:
once in a universe of grass and cornfield

some bird light (and again)
gleamed and the wind took up
the scent of gnawed and broken leaf,

spun it past the cadence in D, began again,
now all meaning beyond the yellow,
the white butterflies, just tied

to the edge of sight by coincidence (coincidence)
the struck and spinning (and again, again)
sound hard and fast like that stiff stalk

stuck in the meadow under all
(and again) the air,
all its light, its butterflies, and again.

Variation 23

a 2 Clav.

Perhaps God is only the left hand, and
the right hand has found a keyboard in a world
we can neither hear nor imagine and

in a variation only unlike this one
with respect to the degree of its being
imaginable is playing now, and other hands,

other hands, as well, playing some part of
some music, hands alternating, for example,
crossing each other's space in the scale (those

spinning butterflies), calling to each other,
conversing, say there are six bears, or nine
bears, and each bear brings a bell to ring

for the sleeping child, and perhaps there is
no sleeping child or less than a sleeping child –
some kind of void that dreams trail into slowly

(for this, despite its flourishes, is a stately music)
and then the bell music plays over the sleep
of sleeping: bell, says one; another, says another,

not yet a bell in the world of the first,
and this music mirrors as stars do fireflies,
as does the rising flame, a great bird.

Variation 24

Canone all'Ottava

In this world, there is no darkness,
no earth, no roots, no hidden tangles
of serpents –

the bass is free, not planted, not framed,
alone in what is not day or night
or even air,

and over it two voices sail, the second
trailing the first by two measures in 9/8,
entering

an octave lower, and it will never catch up.
Remember the church beyond the sunken moon?
It is dark now.

Not an absence of light, but black air: curious stuff,
found only at night, perhaps emitted by gatherings
of toads

(note that stew of trilling) or crickets, themselves
made of black stuff. The sunken moon is a quarter
moon,

about four stories high but impaled in a cornfield
to the depth of one story. This is a sad, upside-down
moon,

its manly eye blinking back tears, lips mumbling
moon babble which has a hint of owl hoot about it.
The moon

is still sinking and the corn stalks lean away.
Silk.   Mouse.   Snake.
Moon tears.

Variation 25

Hansel and Gretel lost in the woods which in the pitch
of night have been turned over, radish plucked, roots

strangling in air. And so we creep chromatically
through this fog of nearly invisible branching.

If there is a moon, it went dark (adagio of adagios).

In a story, both agony of body and suffering of mind,
and behind that, something more terrible than suffering:

Hope. Every dragon in hiding, transformed maiden,
booted rabbit, giant and ogre, numbered or devoured sibling,

treasure of gold (whether egg, harp, coin, or fish) is listening:

The sorcerer and his wedding party, burned inside
his splendid house with the golden basin of blood

and the hacked remains are listening as they burn.
The birds are listening, buried deep in the ground

amid branches and leaves. The roots writhe slowly,

blind in the empty air of night (ascending minor 6ths).
The children lost take steps in haste, then pause and climb.

Finally the dark air begins to thin and light pours up
from what once was earth and now, and now is not,

nor trees nor slow hooded leaves nor moss – silence, then,

and blue above, a white wafer of broken moon, and there –
a little cottage, empty perhaps, but so many paths lead to it –

and the children who wandered hand in hand, not lost now,
hand in hand, somewhere in the pages of the earth.

Variation 26

a 2 Clav.

skeletons of hummingbirds
 dragonflies scrap-heaped
  trills from the meadow
18/16 in the right hand
 cattails in the left
  water's edge at water's edge
a vase
 vase of rabbits
  phosphorescent mice
the asides of squirrels
 cicadas' red-eyed clinking
  wheels
wheels and pounding
 merciless wood violets
  night-scattered breathless
water falling and rilling
 itself twisting itself
  stubbed and smoothed stones
that clatter countlessly
 that   that clatter
  hiding sometimes itself
a small dragon   hellgrammite
 and this rhythm   struck quiet
  passing fence post
traveler it says   traveler
 3/4 in the left hand
  then two travelers perhaps
join hands   traveler
 traveler then
  then the fences fall away
falling falls away
 the giant climbing down
  his lot the acorn's
a last blossoming shower
 of drops set in motion
  past now

past the cadence
    a breath
        wings of washing birds

Variation 27

Canone alla Nona

A step after the octave, a week from tomorrow.
The mailman visits the tiny cottage in the wood,
stepping over the cat on the cobblestones,
deaf to the sounds of breaking sticks from within,

or the clanking of thin blades.
And what does he bring?
Not mushrooms or moon paint,
not the empty envelopes sent by deer or the tomes of owls –

each week then, a single letter –
just that, inside the envelope, a single letter –
this one is *J*.
"What does it mean?" asks the left hand.

"What *does* it mean?" answers the right.
Is it simply that hooded bird? That hooded bird?
The witch (who need not be old, but this one is)
tears the envelope with arthritic fingers.

She is wise now, having given up her beauty and youth,
served herself to time (herself to time),
reads, ponders, understands.
Ponders, understands.

The buried moon will rise like a vine.
The crooked letter leans, teeters, falls.
Crickets.
Crickets cover the moon's thin song

with their own.
With their own.
What does it mean?
Their own song.

Variation 28

In the grand unified theory of trills,
the strong force floats the particles of trill
and gravity holds down the harmonic progression.

Between the two, that ruined moon, of course,
but also, fence posts of sixteenths passing,
filled with the hard weeds of late summer,

the tall grasses tasseled and tufted, torch weed
and thistle, Queen Anne's lace and buttercup, passing,
the old fence and the new, joined each to each,

the wires twisted and warm, the weak force,
and beneath, grasshoppers, snakes, mostly
of the narrow kind – the air's a taste of pollen

and young mouse, cautious in the field under
the ruined moon, by the wood where the children
wander, and in places the land is poor, covered

in a bed of stone where only spiders hide and larks
pass over unwillingly because the air is not the same –
ask the swallows trilling evening's calmed water –

ask the turkey vulture rising in his company
upon a warm fountain welling out of, it would seem,
the very heart of the earth. The trills are measured,

and the fences passing, and the harmony of the earth
is held in the throats and wings, a counterpoint
of toads and crickets and the hiding life, a thin song,

thin as a flame, it might be so, a rising flame.

Variation 29

Do these strings sing a particular silence,
pulling the harpsichord into some fine center –
the well, the stew pot, the particular –

Then strike the key (in G), those bronze levers,
and let loose strings' tolling (confined perhaps
to a certain room) – once in a green kingdom,

the great red king in his lewd delight
pulled down the houses of too many ghosts,
and the floods came, left handed and right,

certain and blind, standing like trees with
legs of bone, of ivory, of keen copper.
And the prince must journey to the east

where the sun soars up from his troves
of drumming gold, and the prince must count
the ghosts, must count himself, some

prince gone before – how many deaths
are written in the bound book of the green
princedom, its wells and stew pots so

still, its trees so juniper – now the prince
returns having heard a sign, the sound
that fled the room where the strings tolled.

What is it? asks the king, the great king,
and the prince cannot remember – *It was the end
of something, of some story. I heard it,*

the prince said, and the king wept, and the
ghosts wept and the clouds above dissolved
that were once ideas, lost children of sound.

Variation 30

Quodlibet

This time, we'll take all the repeats because
the damned moon won't rise without them.

All the paths in the woods are glowing with mice,
and the sound of feathers ruffling,
of forgetting (forgetting) itself. A shadow,

the juniper tree, its comforting roots become stars,
tilts above us, as we settle, once, twice, and finally –

Zipplefagottist, Hundsfott, another dog needing
a bath, bird with a millstone, unmusical joke,
every sound alive in what memory has become,

the dome of heaven with its floating moon –
come closer, treasure the song you've played,

you've heard before, with its fine fit of
puzzle parts, its writhing voices, heavy booted
bass tramping on the ceiling owls' laughter.

A hoot to give that fine bird laboring its
stone wings one last circle one more time.

Aria

(Aria da capo e fine)

Something you've forgotten and almost remembered.
There's a hillside behind you – the mountain has inched
toward the house during these variations and now
it's tipping forward.

The hillside is hidden in deep forest – white pines,
oaks and maples anchoring the deadfall on the steep floor –
grapevines filling in any open spaces – there may be
paths for deer.

There is a constant rain of acorns on the roof – You're alone
in the vat of a dream, all of the stars of the heavens stirred in
with you, and you've heard this music, all music before.
Together

you fall and the world falls so there is no sensation
of falling because the bass line is rising and there are keys
under your fingers. Touch is all that matters.
Somewhere

on the hillside, labyrinthed with deer tracks, there is a stone,
and beneath that stone, everything, music, time itself –
before it became what it appears to be. This is the ghost,
this music,

this appearance, but you're waking, and the hillside
has never been closer – the door might open soundlessly
or offer small complaints, you don't notice – there's the smell
of night,

of owl breath and hanging vines and acorns underfoot,
and in a fern swarmed path, that stone, a glimmer of light
playing,
come from beneath.

NOTES

The epigraphs of the *Walton Poems* are taken from *The Compleat Angler*.

The *Emily Poems* are meditations on individual lines of the following poems of Emily Dickinson: 320, 124, 466, 348, and 584.

DEFINITIONS
Glaver: chatter (14th century)
Malebouche: the voice of evil
Buznack: an old organ, out of tune and playing badly
Beestings: the first milk after a cow has calved
Ratt-Rime: piece of poetry used in charming rats
Lostling: A little person or thing lost
Higgle: to effect by slow degrees
Mirknight: the darkest hour of night
Burdalone: the last child surviving
Bomullock: to make one change one's mirth into sorrow
Larks-leers: any land poor and bare of grass
Knoup: to toll the church-bell
Haspenald: a tall youth, having just shot up
Skainsmate: bawdy companion (from *Romeo and Juliet*)
Dittology: double reading, such as scripture will admit of
Myomancy: divination by means of mice
Mithe: to conceal, to dissemble
Brustle: to make a crackling or rustling noise
Tyromancy: divination by means of cheese

More detailed definitions of these antique words can be found in Joseph T. Shipley's *Dictionary of Early English* and Jeffrey Kacirk's *The Word Museum*.

Knot Poems: Technical information and some quotes came from *The Ashley Book of Knots* by Clifford W Ashley.

Thirteen Ways of Looking at Wallace Stevens are meditations on lines (not necessarily first lines) from Stevens's work.

Goldberg-Variations is based on the structure of Bach's Goldberg–Variations BWV 988.

ACKNOWLEDGMENTS

"Worms," "Feathers," "Who Dreams This Dreams Me," "Unnatural Fishermen," "Flies," and "Monsters," known collectively as Walton Poems, won the 2013 Writers at Work Fellowship (selected by Katherine Coles) and appeared in *Quarterly West*.

"There's a certain slant of light" and "Nor would I be a Poet" appeared in *Vallum: New International Poetics*.

"Glaver" and "Malebouche" appeared in Sugar House Review.

"Buzznack," "Beestings," and "Ratt-Rime" appeared in *Third Wednesday*.

"Haspenald," "Dittology," "Burdalone," and "Tyromancy" appeared in *Subtropics*.

"Skainsmate" appeared in *The Café Review*.

"Mirknight" appeared in *Cider Press Review* and was nominated by the editors for a Pushcart Prize.

"Bomullock" appeared in *FutureCycle*.

"Myomancy" appeared in *Barrow Street*.

"Mithe" and "Brustle" appeared in *Cincinnati Review*.

"Bowline," "Sheepshank," "Clove Hitch," "Cat-o'-Nine-Tails," and "Snarl" appeared in *Theodate*.

"Bell-Ringer's Knot" appeared in *Confrontation*.

The first five sections of "Thirteen Ways of Looking at Wallace Stevens" appeared in *Epoch*.

The last eight of "Thirteen Ways of Looking at Wallace Stevens" appeared in the *Beloit Poetry Journal* and received the 2010 Chad Walsh Prize.

"Variations 4, 9, 20, 22, and 27" appeared in *The Beloit Poetry Journal*. "Variation 22" was nominated by the BPJ editors for a Pushcart Prize.

"Variation 5" appeared in *Cider Press Review*.

'Variations 11, 12, 13, 18, and 23" appeared in *The Literary Review*.

"Variation 10" appeared in *Southern Poetry Review*.

The book was designed by Lesley Landis Designs

Printed in the USA
CPSIA information can be obtained
at www.ICGtesting.com
JSHW082220140824
68134JS00015B/652

9 780932 112729